TRAVEL GUIDE TO TURKEY, ALANYA

2024

By

T.A JOHNSON

TABLE OF CONTENTS

LOCAL ETIQUETTES

CHAPTER 1

INTRODUCTION

Welcome to Alanya, a charming seaside jewel where spectacular natural beauty and rich history meet in perfect harmony. As we set off on this journey using the "Travel Guide to Alanya 2024," you are going to come across a location that captivates the senses, calls forth the spirit of adventure, and makes a lasting impression on the mind.

Located on the Turkish Riviera, Alanya is a timeless blend of the old and the new. While modernity thrives in its bustling bazaars, world-class resorts, and historic fortifications, antiquity is still palpable in the city's winding lanes and medieval fortresses.

Alanya provides a perfect environment for exploration and leisure, with its spectacular Taurus Mountains as a backdrop and sun-kissed beaches lapped by the glittering Mediterranean.
Your key to discovering Alanya's secrets is our guide. Alanya has a lot to offer tourists, whether their goal is to experience the rich history that gives life to historic fortifications like Alanya Castle, learn about the local way of life at the lively Alanya Bazaar, or just savor the delicious flavors of Turkish cuisine.

Take a virtual trip with us through the sights, sounds, and flavors that characterize Alanya in 2024, and get ready to be enchanted with a place that offers adventure, leisure, and a once-in-a-lifetime experience.

Get to know Alanya like never before with the
'Travel Guide to Alanya 2024.' Discover the
mysteries of this alluring Turkish gem, where
breathtaking scenery, culture, and history come
together to offer a once-in-a-lifetime experience.

Take advantage of personal insight to discover
historic castles and fascinating archeological sites.
☐Take pleasure in exhilarating water sports and
unwind on immaculate beaches.
☐ ☐Savor local dishes and delicious Turkish cuisine.
☐ ☐Choose the ideal lodging to fit your style of
travel.
Your journey starts right here! Don't pass up the
chance to add something unique to your trip to
Alanya. To make your trip fantasies come true,
order your copy of "Travel Guide to Alanya 2024"
right away.

Set off on an experience of a lifetime to see how Alanya in 2024 combines old world charm with contemporary luxury. Enjoy delectable cuisine, absorb yourself in the rich history, and soak up the sun on the most breathtaking beaches you've ever seen.

But keep in mind that time passes by without regard to anyone. Travel dreams can come true, so take advantage of this chance to experience the beauty and secrets of Alanya.

So, why do you hesitate? Seize your copy of the "Travel Guide to Alanya2024" and set out on an amazing journey through this idyllic Turkish city. Discover Alanya's riches, make priceless memories, and embark on an adventure of a lifetime. Your journey to Alanya is waiting for you - begin it today!

OVERVIEW OF ALANYA

situated on Turkey's southern coast. Tucked away between the Mediterranean Sea and the Taurus Mountains, this area is renowned for its breathtaking scenery, rich history, and thriving tourism sector. This is a synopsis:

1. Geographical: Alanya is in the province of Antalya and has a Mediterranean climate, meaning that summers are hot and dry and winters are moderate and rainy. Its coastal location offers a variety of rocky cliffs and sandy beaches, while the Taurus Mountains' backdrop creates a striking scene.

2. History: Alanya has a lengthy and rich past that dates back to antiquity. Throughout the Hellenistic, Roman, and Byzantine eras, it was a prominent harbor city.

The most famous is the famous Alanya Castle, which is situated atop a rocky peninsula and was constructed in the thirteenth century by the Seljuks.

3. Tourism: Alanya is a well-liked travel destination because of its stunning beaches, glistening waters, and exciting nightlife. Numerous water sports, boat trips, and other leisure pursuits are available. The town is renowned for its beautifully preserved ancient monuments, such as the Shipyard and the Red Tower.

4. Cuisine: Alanya's Turkish gastronomy is a highlight, with several neighborhood eateries and street sellers serving delectable fare including kebabs, fresh seafood, and classic Turkish desserts. For tourists, dining by the water is a frequent and delightful experience.

5. Economy: With so many hotels, resorts, and other enterprises that serve tourists, Alanya's economy depends heavily on tourism. Additionally, one important economic sector in is agriculture, including the production of fruits and vegetables.

6. Festivals: All year long, Alanya is the site of a number of cultural and entertainment events, such as music festivals, international sporting events, and celebrations of Turkish customs.

7. Transportation: The town is readily reached by car, and Gazipaşa-Alanya Airport, a tiny airport, serves travelers with both domestic and international flights.

Along the Turkish Riviera, Alanya is a charming destination for visitors looking for both relaxation and cultural experiences because of its unique blend of natural beauty, historical legacy, and contemporary conveniences.

WHEN TO VISIT

The ideal time to visit Alanya, a well-known Turkish seaside town, primarily relies on your interests in terms of activities and weather. The weather of Alanya is Mediterranean, with hot, dry summers and warm, rainy winters. Here's a detailed itinerary with times and dates for various kinds of travelers:

1. Summer (June–August)

Climatic conditions: In Alanya, summer is the busiest travel season. Summer temperatures range from 28°C to 35°C (82°F to 95°F). It's ideal for water sports and sunbathing because it's hot and dry.

• **Activities:** For those who enjoy the beach and the ocean, now is the ideal moment. Boat cruises, swimming, and snorkeling are all enjoyable. But be ready for huge crowds.

2. Spring (April - May)

Weather: Springtime temperatures range from 17°C to 25°C (63°F to 77°F), making for nice weather. It's a fantastic time of year for outdoor activities and tourism.

• **Activities:** Discovering Alanya's historical landmarks, such as Alanya Castle, is best done in the spring. The flowering flowers have made the landscape lush and vibrant.

3. Fall (September – November)

Climatic conditions: Autumn brings with it springlike temperatures, with ranges of 20°C to 30°C (68°F to 86°F). It's a more economical and less congested time to go.

• **Activities :** Autumn is a great time to explore local culture and go hiking in the neighboring Taurus Mountains, away from the summer crowd.

Winter (December - February)

Climatic conditions: Alanya experiences moderate winters, with average highs of 10°C to 15°C (50°F to 59°F). It's the off-season, when rain does fall on occasion.

- **Activities:** If you're looking for a more relaxed trip, winter is perfect. Historical sites can still be explored, and the reduced costs make it an affordable choice.

In summary, your preferences will determine the ideal time to visit Alanya. June through August is the best time to visit if you enjoy the beach and the lively summer vibe. Go in the spring or fall for a more balanced experience, with nicer weather and less people. Though less crowded, winters provide cooler temperatures ideal for discovering the town's historical and cultural gems.

HISTORY AND CULTURE

The stunning coastal city of Alanya, Turkey's Antalya Province, boasts a varied and extensive history spanning millennia. Because of how closely its history is entwined with the development and fall of several civilizations, it is an intriguing area to examine.

Ancient History

Although there is Paleolithic evidence of human occupancy in the area, Alanya's written history starts in 1500 BC when it became a part of the Hittite Empire. The city was populated by a number of ancient cultures after the Hittites, such as the Lydians, Cilicians, and Phoenicians.

The Roman Empire's adoption of Alanya in the first century BC was one of the most important moments in the country's history because of its natural beauty.

Medieval Era

The Byzantine Empire took control of the area in the seventh century and continued to have an impact there until the thirteenth. Alanya was essential in the Byzantine Empire's defense against several invaders during this period, including the Arabs and the Seljuk Turks.

Alanya was taken over by Alaeddin Keykubat I's Seljuk Sultanate of Rum in the thirteenth century. The city prospered under his leadership, and as part of its defenses, the famous Red Tower (Kızıl Kule) was constructed. The area was greatly influenced by the Seljuks' architectural and cultural styles.

The Ottoman Rule

Alanya was taken over by the Ottomans in the fourteenth century, and for several centuries afterward it was a part of the Ottoman Empire. Though less prominent in the greater scheme of the empire at this time, Alanya remained a thriving seaside town famed for its trade and agriculture.

Modern Era

Alanya saw profound political transformations together with the rest of Turkey following World

War I and the fall of the Ottoman Empire. Under Mustafa Kemal Atatürk's direction, the Republic of Turkey was founded in 1923. After joining the new country, Alanya grew into a thriving, contemporary metropolis.

Culture

The culture of Alanya is a synthesis of modern and ancient elements. The city is known for its rich musical, dancing, and artistic traditions; Turkish traditional music and dance performances are frequently held there. Because to its seaside position, Alanya's traditional cuisine includes meals like kebabs, pide (Turkish pizza), and numerous seafood delights.

The city's diverse background is reflected in its architectural legacy. Byzantine, Seljuk, and Ottoman buildings can be found, such as the Red Tower, Alanya Castle, and a large number of mosques and churches. With its breathtaking beaches and the Taurus Mountains in the background, Alanya's natural beauty draws visitors from all over the world.

Tourism

Alanya has grown in popularity as a tourist resort in recent decades. It is a popular destination for tourists because of its pleasant Mediterranean climate, historical landmarks, stunning beaches, and a variety of outdoor pursuits like hiking, paragliding, and water sports. From contemporary shopping malls and nightlife to bazaars and local markets, the city provides a blend of traditional and modern services.

The history and culture of Alanya are firmly anchored in its distant past and are influenced by a diverse range of civilizations. Its evolution from a prominent Roman port to a contemporary Turkish metropolis has produced a distinctive and vibrant cultural mosaic that draws tourists from all over the world.

EVENTS AND FESTIVALS:

Alanya celebrates its cultural richness and customs through a range of festivals and events. These annual celebrations offer a chance to immerse oneself in the local way of life and culture. In Alanya, important celebrations and occasions include:

1. International Alanya Jazz Days: This yearly occasion unites jazz fans and gifted musicians from all over the world. Alanya's scenic surroundings are combined with the calming sounds of jazz to provide a unique cultural experience.

2. Alanya International Culture and Art event : This event features traditional music, dance, and art exhibitions among other cultural performances.

It's a fantastic opportunity to experience the local way of life and recognize the artistic abilities of Turkish and foreign artists.

3. Alanya Tourism and Art Festival: This occasion blends artistic pursuits with a focus on boosting tourism in the area. It's a vibrant festival for both locals and visitors, usually featuring a parade, concerts, and exhibitions.

4. Alanya International Bike Festival: This festival is a must-attend for everybody who enjoys outdoor activities. For those who enjoy sports, it's an exciting event with mountain biking, cycling, and other activities.

Economy and industry: Alanya's economy has changed dramatically throughout time. Despite the city's historical reliance on trade and agriculture, tourism is now its main source of income. To meet the demands of travelers, the tourism sector has sparked the creation of a wide range of services, such as lodging, dining options, and transportation.

Agriculture is still significant in the area, which is well-known for producing a wide range of fruits and vegetables, such as pomegranates, citrus fruits, and bananas. Another important industry is fishing, which supplies both locals and visitors with fresh seafood.

Modern Facilities

By creating a state-of-the-art infrastructure, Alanya has responded to its increasing popularity as a travel destination. With highways and an international airport, the city has an extensive and well-connected transportation network. There are many of lodging options, from opulent resorts to affordable hotels, so guests with a variety of tastes and price ranges can find something to suit.

Shopping fans have two options: they can visit contemporary shopping malls with global brands, or they can explore local markets (bazaars) to buy traditional goods and souvenirs. Along with a bustling nightlife, Alanya offers a wide variety of pubs, clubs, and entertainment places.

Preservation of the Environment:

Because of how important it is to preserve Alanya's natural beauty, environmental protection measures have been implemented. The preservation of the Taurus Mountains, the shoreline, and marine life are the main goals of environmental conservation initiatives. Authorities at the local level collaborate with organizations to guarantee that the growth of tourism does not negatively impact the region's natural ecosystems.

Conclusion:

For those looking for a trip that combines history, scenic beauty, and contemporary conveniences, Alanya is a must-visit location because of its rich history, lively culture, and breathtaking scenery. The city provides a unique experience for people who visit its historical places, take part in its festivals, and appreciate its natural surroundings. It is a city that keeps evolving while maintaining its cultural history. Regardless of your interests,history, culture, the great outdoors, or just lounging on the beach,Alanya has something to offer everyone.

CHAPTER 2

GETTING TO ALANYA

To get to Alanya, a popular resort town on the
southern coast of Turkey, you have several options,
depending on your starting point and preferred
mode of transportation. Here are the details for
various ways to reach Alanya:

1. By Air:

- Nearest Airport: The closest major airport to
Alanya is Gazipaşa-Alanya Airport (GZP), located
approximately 45 kilometers (28 miles) from the
town center. Alternatively, you can fly into Antalya
Airport (AYT), which is about 125 kilometers (78
miles) away.

- From International Locations: If you are traveling
internationally, you would typically fly into Antalya

Airport. Several airlines operate flights to Antalya from various destinations. After arriving at Antalya Airport, you can continue your journey to Alanya by other means, such as bus, taxi, or private transfer.

   - Domestic Flights: If you are already in Turkey, you can check for domestic flights to Gazipaşa-Alanya Airport. These flights are available from major cities like Istanbul and Ankara.

2. By Bus:

   - If you prefer a cost-effective option: you can take a bus to Alanya. Turkish cities are well-connected by an extensive bus network. You can find buses departing from major cities like Antalya, Istanbul, and Ankara. Bus travel is affordable and comfortable, with various bus companies offering services.

3. By Car:

  - If you enjoy road trips and want the flexibility to explore the region: you can rent a car. Alanya is accessible by road, and you can reach it via the D400 coastal highway if you're coming from the west (Antalya) or east (Gazipaşa).

4. By Boat:

  - Alanya has a marina, and you can also reach it by boat if you're traveling along the Turkish coast or arriving via a cruise ship. The marina offers facilities for those arriving by sea.

5. By Train:

  - While Turkey has a developing high-speed rail network, there is no direct train service to Alanya. However, you can take a train to nearby cities like Antalya or Mersin and continue your journey to Alanya by bus or other means.

6. By Taxi or Private Transfer:

- If you prefer convenience and don't want to deal with public transportation, you can arrange for a taxi or a private transfer to take you directly to Alanya from the airport or your current location.

Make sure to plan your trip well in advance, considering your budget, travel preferences, and the season you are visiting, as Alanya is a popular tourist destination, especially during the summer months.

Alanya, a popular tourist destination in Turkey, has a couple of transportation options:

1. Gazipasa Airport (IATA: GZP): This is the nearest airport to Alanya, located about 40 kilometers (25 miles) from the city center. It primarily serves domestic and a few international flights.

2. Antalya Airport (IATA: AYT): While not in Alanya itself, Antalya Airport is the main international gateway to the region. It's about 125 kilometers (78 miles) from Alanya and provides a wider range of flight options.

As for ports, Alanya does not have a major commercial port. However, the region has several smaller marinas and yacht harbors that cater to recreational boating and sailing.

Please note that the availability of transportation options may change over time, so it's a good idea to check with airlines and local authorities for the most up-to-date information.

ACCOMODATION

Situated on Turkey's southern shore, Alanya provides a diverse array of lodging choices to accommodate a range of spending limits and inclinations. Below is a comprehensive list of places to stay in Alanya:

1. Hotels: -

Luxury Hotels: Alanya is home to a number of upscale lodging options with first-rate amenities and breathtaking views of the sea. The Adam & Eve Hotel, Eftalia Aqua Resort, and Vogue Hotel Supreme are a few well-known luxury lodging options.

Mid-Range Hotels: There are lots of mid-range hotels that offer cozy lodgings at affordable prices. Take into account choices such as the Kleopatra Bebek Hotel, Sunprime C-Lounge Hotel, and Dizalya Palm Garden Hotel.

Budget Hotels: Alanya offers reasonably priced lodging options for those on a tight budget, including the Wien Hotel, My Home Apart, and the En Vie Beach Boutique Hotel.

2. Motels: - Compared to hotels, motels in Alanya tend to be more modest and affordable. These are the best options for tourists seeking a basic place to stay. The Adenya Hotel & Resort and the Montebello Resort Motel are two examples.

3. Resorts: - Alanya has a range of beachside all-inclusive resorts. The Kirman Arycanda De Luxe, Club Hotel Falcon, and Delphin Deluxe Resort are a few well-liked choices.

4. Vacation Rentals: The market for vacation rentals, which include villas and apartments, is expanding in Alanya. Listings in Alanya can be found on websites such as Booking.com, Vrbo, and Airbnb, which are good for larger parties or families looking for more privacy and space.

5. Budget-friendly Stays: - Alanya offers several of choices for tourists on a tight budget:

- **Hostels:** For travelers, hostels like Alanya Youth Hostel and Castle Hostel are ideal.

Pensions. For a reasonably priced and genuine experience, think about booking a room at one of the neighborhood pensions, like the Alantur Hotel or the Yalcin Hotel.

- **Campsites:** For a stay in the outdoors, campers can check out Alanya Camping and Olympos Lodge.

6. Boutique Accommodations: - For those seeking a distinctive and customized experience, Alanya also offers quaint boutique hotels like the Blue Night Hotel, Villa Sonata, and Azura Villas.

It is advisable to reserve lodging well in advance during the busiest travel period, which usually spans from late spring to early autumn. Prices can change according on the season, therefore it's wise to check reviews to find the ones that fits perfectly into your budget or to your preference.

ATTRACTIONS

Travelers are drawn to Alanya, a mesmerizing treasure on Turkey's Mediterranean coast, by its abundance of historical, natural, and cultural attractions. Set against the Taurus Mountains, this enchanted town is a mosaic of historic defenses, immaculate beaches, and lively bazaars. Alanya offers a wide range of captivating activities for anyone seeking relaxation, exploration of natural history, or both. Come along as we explore the amazing sights and activities that characterize this idyllic seaside town and learn why Alanya is a place that guarantees a once-in-a-lifetime experience.

1. Alanya Castle: One of the city's most recognizable landmarks is Alanya Castle. It has breathtaking panoramic views of the Mediterranean Sea and is situated atop a rocky slope.

The castle is a magnificent example of Seljuk architecture, having been built in the thirteenth century. It is made up of different gates, towers, and walls, each having a special historical significance. Within the castle complex, visitors can explore the well-preserved fortress walls, climb the Red Tower for even more picturesque views, and tour the famous Sultan Suleiman Mosque.

2. The Beach of Cleopatra: Popular Cleopatra's Beach is renowned for its magnificent golden beaches and pristine waters. It is reported that during her visit to Alanya, Cleopatra herself went swimming here.

- There are many other facilities at the beach, such as sun loungers, umbrellas, and water sports. - The beach is kept up nicely. The little, polished pebbles that are thought to have been transported from Egypt—possibly by Cleopatra herself—are what make this beach special.

3. Damlatas Cave : Close to Cleopatra's Beach, Damlatas Cave is a natural treasure. It is well-known for its striking stalagmite and stalactite formations. Because of the high humidity and the discharge of trace elements from the rocks, the cave is also well-known for its healing microclimate, which is thought to aid with respiratory issues. Take a guided tour to discover the fascinating geological structures inside the cave and discover its special therapeutic qualities.

4. Red Tower: - Located in the port, the Red Tower, also called Kızıl Kule, is a well-known landmark in Alanya. Constructed around the 13th century, the tower functioned as a fortification and a location to keep ship supplies.

A museum featuring artifacts from Alanya's past, including Seljuk and Ottoman periods, is currently housed in the Red Tower.

5. Alanya Archaeological Museum: Explore the rich history of the area by visiting the Alanya Archaeological Museum. It holds an eclectic assortment of relics, like as sculptures, ceramics, and inscriptions that shed light on Alanya's prehistoric history. For individuals who are interested in local culture and history, the museum is a wonderful place to visit.

I suggest using a map or travel app, or stopping by a local tourist office when you get to Alanya for photos and comprehensive directions. They are able to provide you current instructions and details on how to get to these places.

ACTIVITIES IN ALANYA

The charming coastal town of Alanya, located in southern Turkey on the Mediterranean Sea, has a wide variety of activities to suit a wide range of interests and tastes.

Alanya, tucked away between the untamed Taurus Mountains and the turquoise Mediterranean, offers a singular combination of historical significance and scenic beauty.

Every traveler's heart can be captured by Alanya's stunning beaches, exciting nightlife, historical landmarks, and mouthwatering cuisine. We will go over the fascinating things to do in Alanya in this introduction, which is a must-visit location for anyone looking for the ideal balance of leisure, adventure, and cultural discovery.

1. Water Sports:

- Time: The greatest time to enjoy water sports is in the warm months, which is usually May through October.

- Directions: Water sports activities are available at several of Alanya's beaches. Damlatas Beach and Kleopatra Beach are well-liked options.

- sports: You have access to jet skiing, parasailing, windsurfing, paddleboarding, and scuba diving among other sports. Typically, these are open from early in the morning until late in the afternoon.

2. Boat trips:

- season: Although boat trips are typically offered in Alanya year-round, the optimum season is in the summer, when the weather is favorable.

- Directions: The majority of boat cruises depart from Alanya's harbor. Along the seaside, travel operators are widely accessible.

- Tour Types: Numerous boat cruises are available, such as fishing excursions, yacht tours, and pirate ship tours. These tours can take hours or even a day.

3. Hiking and Nature Trails:

- Time: When the weather isn't too hot, spring and autumn are the ideal seasons to enjoy hiking and nature trails. Best time to visit is the month of April - June and September - November.

- Directions: There are several hiking trails in Alanya. The Alanya Castle, Sapadere Canyon, and Dim River Valley are a few well-known examples.

- Guided tours: You can sign up for guided hiking trips or explore these routes yourself. Depending on the itinerary, these tours might run for many hours and typically begin in the morning.

4. Entertainment and Nightlife:

- Time: The majority of bars and clubs are open late into the early hours of the morning, Alanya has a lively nightlife from late May to early September. .

- Directions: Alanya's main nightlife district is located along the main street and surrounding the port. .

- alternatives: There's a variety of entertainment alternatives in Alanya, such as bars by the beach, clubs, live music venues, and even outdoor parties. Usually starting at around 10 p.m., the action lasts into the early hours of the morning.

Please be aware that local laws and weather patterns can affect these activities' availability. When planning a vacation to Alanya, it's a good idea to inquire about the most recent information and timetables with local tour operators and venues.

CHAPTER 3
DINNING AND CUISINE

Dinning in Alanya is an adventure through Mediterranean cuisine, where the lively culture and lengthy history of Turkey come together on your plate. It's more than just a gourmet experience. Alanya's cuisine is a celebration of taste, a blend of tradition and creativity that makes an everlasting impression on your mouth. Dishes range from scorching kebabs to fresh seafood, savory mezes, and sweet baklava. You will find that every meal here is an opportunity to fully experience the essence of this alluring destination, and every dish is a revelation as you explore this coastal town.

Come along on a culinary journey through the superb dining and cuisine of Alanya, where each dish showcases the region's art of cooking and its kind, welcoming vibe.

1) ALANYA'S TURKISH FOOD: Alanya Turkish food scene is thriving, providing foodies with a delightful culinary adventure. The cuisine is profoundly entrenched in heritage and embraced by innovation. The richness of Turkish flavors and the influence of the Mediterranean are evident in Alanya's culinary scene, which produces a lively and varied cuisine.

Turkish cuisine is arguably best known for its kebabs, of which Alanya offers some of the best.

The options are infinite, ranging from tasty shish kebabs to luscious Adana kebabs made with spicy minced meat and the delicious doner, which is grilled to perfection.

Meze is a delightful start to any dinner, consisting of a variety of tiny, savory appetizers. These appetizers are ideal for sharing with friends and family because they include ingredients like fresh veggies, olive oil, herbs, and a variety of dips.

With all of the Mediterranean's richness at their fingertips, seafood lovers will be in heaven. When prepared with skill, locally caught fish and seafood are a true sensory experience. Calamari, shrimp, and grilled fish are just a few of the mouthwatering options you may eat near the sea.

Try the gözleme, a savory pastry stuffed with cheese, spinach, or other ingredients, or pide, a pizza prepared in the Turkish style.

Enjoy kunefe, a warm, cheesy delight drowned in syrup, or baklava, a sweet, layered pastry, for dessert.

Turkish food will entice you as you visit Alanya's lively bazaars and neighborhood eateries. You will experience the harmony of tastes, the warmth of Turkish hospitality, and the real spirit of this stunning Mediterranean town with every bite.

2) WELL-KNOWN EATERIES: These are a few of the well-known eateries in Alanya, Turkey, as of January 2023, the last time I checked. Please be aware that restaurant trends might change over time, and that since then, new establishments can have opened. When visiting Alanya, it's a good idea to look at the most recent reviews and get advice from the locals.

Sultan Sofrasi is well-known for its traditional Turkish food and stunning views of Alanya Castle.

2. Alanya Harbor Restaurant: Located next to the marina, this eatery has a terrific atmosphere and serves a range of seafood specialties.

3. Keyif Restaurant: A little eatery featuring a broad menu that includes Turkish and foreign fare.

4. Kale Panorama Restaurant: Offering stunning views and a variety of Turkish and Mediterranean meals, this restaurant is close to Alanya Castle.

5. Antique Restaurant: This restaurant serves a blend of Turkish and international cuisine in a warm, historically inspired setting.

6. The Harbour Resto Lounge: This vibrant restaurant with a bustling atmosphere is located near the port and serves fresh seafood.

7. Istanbul Restaurant: Located in the center of Alanya and well-known for its kebabs and Turkish dishes.

8. Large Alanya Restaurant: Exceptionally large sea vistas and a combination of Turkish and international dishes.

9. Vanilla Restaurant: This seaside eatery serves a range of Turkish and Mediterranean dishes.

10. Saray Restaurant: renowned for its traditional Turkish food and rooftop dining area with magnificent views.

3) STREET FOOD AND LOCAL DELICACIES.

Like many Turkish towns, Alanya provides a mouthwatering selection of street and local delicacies that are authentically representative of the region's culinary tradition.

In Alanya, you should definitely taste these street and indigenous foods:

1. Kebab Doner: Slices of seasoned meat, usually lamb or chicken, are roasted on a vertical rotisserie in this traditional Turkish dish. Usually, it is served with fresh vegetable dips and sauces made of yogurt inside a flatbread.

2. Kumpir : Kumpir is a well-liked street meal that consists of mashed baked potatoes topped with cheese, corn, olives, and other toppings.

3. Simit: Also called "Turkish bagel," simit is a sesame-seed-crusted ring-shaped bread. Popular as a snack, it's frequently served with tea.

4. Lahmacun: Also known as "Turkish pizza," lahmacun is a thin, circular flatbread that is topped with a blend of spices, veggies, and minced meat. It's a tasty and convenient snack.

5. Midye Dolma: These are mussels that have been stuffed with a spiced rice, herb, and vegetable mixture. They are sold at seaside booths and are typically served with a squeeze of lemon.

6. Manti: Turkish dumplings, usually covered with tomato sauce and yogurt and filled with ground meat or veggies. For those seeking a distinctive regional flavor, they are an absolute must-try.

7. Pide: Often referred to as "Turkish pizza," pide is a flatbread fashioned like a boat topped with cheese, veggies, and minced meat, among other toppings.

8. Cig Kofte: Popular among the natives are these uncooked meatballs and spicy bulgur. Usually, they are served with a squeeze of lemon, fresh greens, and a wrap.

9. Gozleme: a delicious thin-dough pastry from Turkey packed with cheese, minced meat, spinach, or other fillings. It's folded in half after cooking on a griddle.

10. Dondurma: Turkish ice cream, distinguished by its distinct, stretchy texture, is frequently offered by street sellers in an amusing manner.

A wonderful way to really experience Alanya's culinary culture and appreciate the flavors of this stunning seaside town is to sample some of the street cuisine and dishes that are served there.

SHOPPING IN ALANYA

Shopping in Alanya, a well-known vacation town on Turkey's Mediterranean coast, provides a lovely blend of contemporary malls, traditional bazaars, and locally made goods. Here's an overview of Alanya shopping, whether you're looking for handicrafts, apparel, spices, or souvenirs:

1. Markets and Bazaars: You should definitely visit Alanya's traditional markets and bazaars. You can negotiate for a wide range of things, such as textiles, apparels ,spices,fresh vegetables and spices at the always busy Alanya Bazaar. For local items, it's also most beneficial checking out the Market on Friday.

2. Turkish Kilims and Carpets: Turkey is well-known for its beautiful kilims and carpets that are created by hand. These exquisite and lovely works of art can be found in a number of Alanya's stores.

3. Gold and Jewelry: The extensive collection of gold and jewelry at Alanya's Gold Center is well-known. Turkish jewelry frequently has one-of-a-kind patterns and precious stones.

4. Leather Goods: Alanya is an excellent location to purchase leather goods such as purses, shoes, and jackets. The town is filled with leather shops.

5. Spices and Turkish Delights: Alanya is full of spice shops that sell a wide variety of aromatic spices, teas, and Turkish delight, a well-liked sweet treat from the area.

6. Local Souvenirs : Seek up mementos that showcase the customs and traditions of the area, like ceramic ceramics, evil eye amulets, and Turkish coffee sets.

7. Shopping Malls: Alanya offers a number of malls, including Megamall and Alanyum Shopping Center, if you'd want a more contemporary shopping experience. These shopping centers provide a variety of foreign and Turkish brands.

8. Handicrafts: Don't pass up the chance to peruse stores that provide handcrafted goods including fabrics, glassware, and pottery.

9. Local Food Products: A range of Turkish cheeses, honey, and olive oil are among the delectable offerings of Alanya. These are excellent edible mementos.

10. Antiques: Some of Alanya's antique stores may have one-of-a-kind items if you're interested in antiquing.

In traditional marketplaces, be ready for some friendly haggling; nevertheless, fixed prices are more typical in malls and retail establishments. Remember that local markets frequently have some of the finest bargains, so take your time exploring and soaking up Alanya's vibrant retail scene.

BAZAARS AND MARKETS

There are a number of active markets and bazaars in Alanya where you may shop for a wide range of things, take in the colorful atmosphere, and become immersed in the local way of life. Here are a few of Alanya's well-known marketplaces and bazaars:

1. The Alanya Bazaar : is one of the busiest and most well-known marketplaces in Alanya. Situated in the center of the town, it provides a broad selection of goods, such as apparel, fabrics, spices, fresh fruit, and mementos. Here is where you can bargain for the finest deals.

2. Cuma Pazarı Friday Market: This outdoor market, happens every Friday, it's a great area to explore. You can get any Fresh household produce you want. It's a great area to savour the atmosphere of a market in neighborhood.

3. Alanya Fish Market (Balık Pazarı) : This market, which is close to the harbor, is a seafood lover's dream come true. Fresh fish can be purchased and cooked at one of the neighboring eateries. It's an excellent spot for a seafood lunch.

4. Mahmutlar Bazaar: Don't miss Alanya's weekly bazaar if you're in the Mahmutlar neighborhood. It's a fantastic area to purchase locally produced items and produce, and it resembles the Friday Market.

5. Sarapsa Han Bazaar: Located in a caravanserai from the Ottoman era, this historic market provides a distinctive shopping experience. In a quaint environment, traditional Turkish carpets, fabrics, and handcrafted products are available.

6. Keykubat Bazaar: Situated in the Keykubat neighborhood, this market is a little more subdued than the main Alanya Bazaar but nevertheless provides a wide range of goods, including as apparel, spices, and regional handicrafts.

7. Oba Bazaar: Vegetables, fruits apparels, and household goods are all sold there at the market situated in the Oba area. If you're planning to stay here, it's perfect.

8. Farmers' Markets: You may purchase fresh, locally produced products at a number of smaller farmers' markets in Alanya in addition to the big markets.

Plan your visit properly as many of these markets are very busy in the mornings and early afternoons. Discovering these markets is a great way to experience Alanya's beautiful and genuine culture in addition to shopping.

HANDICRAFTS AND SOUVENIRS

A vast selection of handicrafts and souvenirs that showcase the creativity and culture of the region can be found in Alanya. When you visit Alanya, think about acquiring these distinctive souvenirs:

1. Evil Eye Amulets: In Turkey, the evil eye, also known as "nazar boncuk," is a well-known emblem that is said to fend against bad energy. Amulets, keychains, and jewelry with the recognizable blue and white eye motif are available.

2. Ceramics: Ornamental plates, bowls, and intricate tiles are just a few examples of the many forms that traditional Turkish ceramics take. These are frequently painted by hand with vibrant, detailed designs.

3. Turkish Kilims and Carpets: Turkey is well known for its beautiful kilims and carpets that are created by hand. These exquisitely made rugs come in an assortment of patterns and dimensions.

4. Turkish Tea Sets: Turkish tea culture permeates everyday existence. Think of buying a tea set, which comes with exquisite teapot and elaborate glasses.

5. Copperware: Commonly seen in Alanya's markets are copper objects like as decorations, platters, and coffee pots. They are attractive mementos because of the fine workmanship and beautiful designs.

6. Spices and Turkish Delights: Get a variety of flavorful spices and Turkish pleasure, a delicious dessert that comes in a variety of flavors like pomegranate, rose, and pistachio.

7. Leather Products: Shoes, belts, bags, coats, and other leather accessories are among Alanya's best-known products. Turkish leather is well known for its great quality.

8. Local Art and Paintings: Look for paintings and artwork that perfectly reflect the essence of Alanya's stunning buildings and scenery by visiting local art galleries.

9. Handmade Jewelry: Look through jewelry stores to find one-of-a-kind items with traditional Turkish motifs and semi-precious gemstones.

10. Local Food Products and Olive Oil: Since Alanya is surrounded by olive trees, make sure to sample and purchase locally produced olive oil.

Other regional specialties including honey, jams, and dried fruits are also available.

11. Turkish Calligraphy: The art of Turkish calligraphy is quite complex. Seek for calligraphy prints, particularly those that have insightful words and ideas.

12. Ceramic Lamps: Various sized and colored ceramic lamps are attractive and useful mementos.

While shopping in Alanya for souvenirs and handicrafts, keep in mind that although fixed prices are standard in more established stores and boutiques, haggling is typical in markets. Spend some time browsing the many stores and booths to get the ideal keepsakes to remember your trip to this lovely Turkish town.

SHOPPING STREETS

There are numerous retail avenues in Alanya where you may go shopping and discover a large selection of goods. The following are a some of Alanya's well-known shopping avenues:

1. Atatürk Boulevard: One of Alanya's main thoroughfares, Atatürk Boulevard is dotted with a variety of stores, cafes, and eateries. It is a well-liked location for people-watching and shopping.

2. İskele Street: Situated close to the harbor, skele Street is well-known for its stores that offer apparel, souvenirs, and handcrafted items. You can find some really interesting presents and mementos there.

3. Cumhuriyet Street: Full of shops offering apparel, accessories, jewelry, and more, this bustling street is located in the heart of the city. It's a center for fashionable goods and fashion.

4. Oba Street: In the Oba neighborhood, Oba Street is a fantastic spot to buy for locally made goods and everyday essentials. Compared to other streets in the city center, it is a little less crowded with tourists.

The Saray Mahallesi (Palace District) is a lovely neighborhood in the center of Alanya with boutique shops selling a variety of goods, from handicrafts to clothes.

6. Barbaros Street : Known for its stores, cafes, and restaurants, Barbaros Street is located next to the Damlataş Cave. This is a nice place to explore and you can find a variety of stuff here.

7. Obagöl Caddesi : This street, which is a part of the Obagöl neighborhood, has a variety of shops, such as jewelry and clothes stores.

8. Keykubat Caddesi: Particularly in the Keykubat neighborhood, Keykubat Street offers a wide range of stores. You can look through local products, accessories, and apparel.

Make sure to check out the local bazaars and markets, particularly if you're looking for genuine Turkish goods and a more traditional shopping experience. Have fun on your Alanya shopping excursions!

DAY TRIPS AND EXCURSIONS

Visitors may enjoy a range of thrilling day tours and excursions from Alanya, a stunning coastal town in Turkey. Here are a few well-liked choices:

1. Alanya Castle: Take a tour of Alanya Castle, which is atop a hill with a view of the town, to begin your day. Admire the expansive views of the Mediterranean Sea while touring the medieval stronghold.

2. Cleopatra Beach: Recline on the lovely golden beaches and glistening blue seas of Cleopatra Beach for a tranquil day. Thinking about swimming when you are out there is an excellent choice and location.

3. Dim Cave and Dimcay River: Discover the amazing stalactites and stalagmites in the enthralling Dim Cave, a natural wonder. After that, take a boat ride or have dinner beside the Dimcay River.

4. Alanya Aqua Park: An enjoyable visit if you're traveling with family is the Alanya Aqua Park. It offers pools, water slides, and family-friendly entertainment.

5. Pirate Boat Cruise: Take a boat ride over Alanya's coastline with a pirate theme. Delectable meals are all available on board this includes snorkeling an swimming as well.

6. Sapadere Canyon : Explore the verdant Sapadere Canyon, a tranquil natural area featuring hiking paths and waterfalls. It provides a wonderful natural hideaway.

7. Jeep Safari: Explore the Taurus Mountains, stop by traditional villages, and take in the breathtaking scenery with an exhilarating jeep safari.

8. Manavgat Waterfall : Just a short drive from Alanya, this picturesque location is perfect for a picnic and a refreshing swim.

9. Aspendos Theater : See one of the best-preserved Roman theaters in the world, Aspendos Theater, and if it's open, take in a live performance.

10. Side Day Trip: Spend a day visiting Side, another historic town with ancient ruins, a gorgeous harbor, and a charming old town. Always check the availability and schedules of these excursions, and take your interests into consideration when organizing your day trips in Alanya. Whether you're more interested in history, nature, or adventure, Alanya has something to offer everyone.

Popular nearby destinations to visit include:

1. Pamukkale:

- Location: Situated in southwest Turkey, Pamukkale is a unique natural wonder. - Attractions:

- Cotton Castle: Known for its terraces of white, mineral-rich thermal waters that cascade down the mountainside, resembling a "cotton castle." These terraces are formed by calcium deposits from the hot springs.

- Hierapolis: Adjacent to Pamukkale is the ancient Roman city of Hierapolis, with well-preserved ruins that include a theater, necropolis, and Cleopatra's Pool, where visitors can swim in ancient Roman thermal baths.

- Activities: Visitors can stroll around the travertine terraces, explore the archaeological site of Hierapolis, and unwind in the thermal waters.

2. Cappadocia:

- Location: Known for its unique scenery, Cappadocia is a surreal region in central Turkey.

Actractions: - Fairy Chimneys: Cappadocia is well-known for its unusual rock formations, which are colloquially called "fairy chimneys." Houses, churches, even underground cities have been carved out of these.

-Hot Air Balloon Rides: With its stunning views of the surreal landscape, Cappadocia is one of the top sites in the world for hot air balloon rides.

- Göreme Open-Air Museum: Magnificent frescoes can be found inside rock-cut churches at this UNESCO World Heritage site.

- Activities: Take a hot air balloon flight for a bird's-eye view of the area, stroll through the valleys, and explore cave homes.

3. Antalya:

- Location: Antalya is a bustling coastal city in southern Turkey.

- Attractions:

- Old Town (Kaleiçi): Discover the old town with its quaint cobblestone streets, Ottoman-era architecture, and the ancient Hadrian's Gate. - Beaches: Antalya has many lovely beaches, where you can unwind and swim.

 - Antalya Museum: See artifacts from the region's history at this impressive archaeological museum.

-Activities: Take a stroll through the old town, engage in water sports, and visit the Düden Waterfalls.

4. Aspendos: Aspendos is an ancient city in southern Turkey, not far from Antalya.

- Attractions: - Aspendos Theater: One of the outstanding specimens of its type, this ancient Roman theater has been extraordinarily well maintained. Performances still take place there nowadays.

- Agora: Take a tour of the remains of the aqueduct, agora, and marketplace.

- Activities: Take in a trip to the archaeological site and the theater.

These locations provide a wide variety of experiences, ranging from ancient sites in Aspendos and the coastal beauty of Antalya to natural wonders in Pamukkale and Cappadocia. Each location in Turkey has it's own charm this makes it fascinating tourist center.

PRACTICAL INFORMATION

Nestled on Turkey's southern coast is the well-known resort town of Alanya. To help you make the most of your stay, here are some useful details:

1. Getting There: The two airports that offer flights to Alanya are Gazipasa, 45 minutes from the town, and Antalya, 2 hours distance. Alanya is also accessible by vehicle or bus.

2. Weather: Due to its Mediterranean climate, Alanya experiences hot, dry summers and warm, wet winters. It's adviseable to visit during fall or spring as they are the best seasons to visit.

3. Hotels: There are many different types of lodging available in Alanya, ranging from luxurious resorts to affordable hotels. Booking your stay in advance during the busiest travel times is a smart idea.

4. Transportation: Taxis, buses, and dolmus (shared minibuses) are convenient ways to get around Alanya. If you'd want more freedom, you can also rent a car.

5. Currency: The Turkish Lira (TRY) is the currency used in Turkey. Although most places accept credit cards, it's a good idea to have extra cash on hand for minor purchases and local markets.

6. Language: English and other European languages are spoken in tourist areas, while Turkish is the official language.

7. Local Cuisine: Turkish delight, baklava, and kebabs are just a few of the mouthwatering Turkish delicacies available in Alanya. Try the classic Turkish coffee and tea; you won't regret it.

8. Activities: Alanya offers a plethora of outdoor activities, including hiking, boat trips, and water sports; it is also a historical site with a vibrant nightlife.

9. Cultural Respect: Dress modestly when visiting mosques or religious sites; additionally, it is courteous to take off your shoes when entering someone's home.

10. Safety: Although Alanya is generally safe for tourists, it is advisable to exercise common sense caution by protecting your belongings and being aware of your surroundings. Remember to check for any updated travel advisories or entry requirements prior to your trip, as these can change. Enjoy your visit to Alanya!

BANKING AND CURRENCY IN ALANYA

The Turkish Lira (TRY), like the rest of Turkey, is the country's official currency. Here are some details regarding money and banking in Alanya:

1. Currency Exchange: Banks, exchange offices (döviz bürosu), and certain hotels accept foreign currencies, including US dollars and euros, in exchange for Turkish Lira. Because currency values fluctuate, it's essential to compare prices to find the greatest offer.

2. ATMs: You can find ATMs all across Alanya, and most of them allow you to take out Turkish Lira. To avoid any issue with your credit or debit card when traveling, let your bank be made aware of your travel plans.

3. Credit Cards: Visa, MasterCard, and other credit cards are widely accepted in Alanya, particularly in larger shops, restaurants, and hotels. That being said, you should always bring cash for smaller establishments, markets, or locations that may not take credit cards.

4. Banking Hours: Banks in Alanya are normally open Monday through Friday from 9:00 AM to 5:00 PM, with some branches opening late on Saturdays.

5. Traveler's Checks: These days, traveler's checks are less common. It might become problematic later. Instead, you should rely on ATMs and credit cards for your financial needs.

6. Currency Exchange Apps: Having a currency conversion app on your smartphone is also a smart option for easy access. By doing so, you may make sure you're receiving a fair exchange rate and better comprehend rates.

7. Tipping: In Alanya, leaving a gratuity is customary and highly valued for excellent service. It is traditional to leave a gratuity in restaurants, usually 10%. Tipping hotel employees, tour guides, and cab drivers is also considered courteous.

To avoid any problems with your cards, don't forget to let your bank know about your trip schedule. Even while many establishments take cards, keeping extra cash on hand is advisable, particularly for smaller purchases and in farther-flung locations.

LANGUAGE IN ALANYA

Like the rest of Turkey, Alanya has Turkish as its official language.

Here are some details regarding the Alanyan language:

1. Turkish Script: Since Turkish is written in Latin, it is comparatively comprehensible to speakers of other languages that employ the Latin alphabet. You can see it written in this script on menus, official documents, and road signs.

2. English: A lot of people in Alanya speak English, particularly in the tourist districts, hotels, restaurants, and retail establishments. Try as much as you can to relate well with them when speaking as alot of the people in the tourism business can converse in English.

3. Other Languages: Although English and Turkish are the most often spoken languages in Alanya, you can also hear speakers of other European languages including German and Russian because of the city's diversified visitors.

4. Learning a Few Basic Turkish Phrases: Although not required, knowing a few fundamental Turkish phrases will improve your encounters and conversations with locals. Sayings such as "Teşekkür ederim" (thank you), "Evet" (yes), and "Merhaba" (hello) can be useful.

5. Signage: To facilitate tourists' navigation of the city, a lot of store signs, street signs, and information on public transportation are posted in both Turkish and English.

Though most of your demands in Alanya, especially in the tourist districts, can be met with English, locals appreciate it when visitors try to pick up a few polite Turkish phrases.

HEALTH AND SAFETY ADVICE

When visiting Alanya, safety and health are important factors to take into account. Here are some pointers to guarantee a secure and well-being visit:

SAFETY ADVICE:

1. General Safety: Travelers can feel somewhat safe visiting Alanya. But proceed with the same prudence as you would in any other city. Keep an eye on your surroundings, take care of your possessions, and refrain from showing off priceless stuff.

2. Health Insurance: Make sure your trip insurance includes coverage for medical costs. Acquaint oneself with the nearby medical facilities and maintain a contact list for emergencies.

3. Water: While tap water is usually safe to drink in Alanya, you might want to consider bottled water if you have a sensitive stomach. When drinking and brushing your teeth, use bottled water.

4. Food Safety: While Turkish food is excellent, exercise caution while purchasing from street vendors. Eat in famous eateries with lots of customers as that means the place is safe for eating.

5. Sun Protection: Due to its Mediterranean environment, Alanya experiences intense sun exposure. To prevent sunburn and other heat-related problems, wear a hat, use sunscreen, and drink plenty of water.

6. Swimming Safety: Although Alanya's beaches are well-liked, always pay attention to caution flags and abide by lifeguard guidelines. When swimming, pay attention to undersea risks and currents.

Health Advice:

1. Vaccinations: Make sure your usual vaccinations are current with your healthcare physician before to travel. It can be advised to get additional vaccines based on your schedule.

2. Mosquito Protection: Mosquitoes might be bothersome during certain seasons. Insect repellent and mosquito netting are recommended, particularly if you are lodging in an open-air setting.

3. Medical Facilities: There are a number of clinics and hospitals in Alanya, although the standard of care varies. Finding the closest medical institution to your lodging is a smart idea.

4. Prescription Medications: Make sure you bring enough of your prescription drugs with you for the duration of your vacation. Keep a copy of your prescription with them, along with their original packaging.

5. Traveler's Diarrhea: Just in case, bring over-the-counter drugs to treat diarrhea. Practice good hand hygiene and use caution when consuming food and liquids.

6. Travel First Aid Kit: Pack a simple first aid bag that includes bandages, painkillers, and any prescription drugs you might require.

7. Emergency Services : Acquaint yourself with Alanya's emergency phone numbers. For medical emergencies, the global emergency number is 112.

You can travel to Alanya with peace of mind and make the most of your time in this stunning Turkish resort by adhering to these safety and health recommendations.

LOCAL ETIQUETTES

It is imperative to observe local customs and etiquette when traveling to Alanya, or any other foreign location. The following advice relates to Alanya local etiquette:

1. Greetings: Saying "Merhaba" (Hello) or "Selam" (Hi) to new acquaintances is a polite way to strike up a discussion. Same genders in this areas usually shake hands as greetings. When you are talking to someone in a formal setting, make use of "Bay" for Mr. and "Bayan" for Mrs. or Miss.

2. Modesty: Alanya is a tourist attraction, but it belongs to a nation that practices conservatism. Dress modestly when you visit mosques or other places of worship. Both men and women should dress so that their knees are covered, and women should cover their shoulders.

3. Shoes: When visiting someone's home, it is traditional to take off your shoes. To find out if this is normal, look for a stack of shoes close to the door.

4. Respect for Elders: Treat senior citizens with dignity. When an elderly person enters a room, it is considered courteous to stand and offer your seat.

5. Public Expressions of Affection: try to minimize the use of public show of affection. Public show of affection like kissing, hugging , and locking hands might not go down well in a more traditional setting or area .

6. Hospitality: Turkish people are known for their friendly nature and kindness. It's their culture to offer little gifts, like flowers or chocolates, to the host when you are invited to their homes.

7. Tipping: In Alanya, giving of tips is a culture. It's important to know the percentage to tip as most people tip up to ten percent.

For providing good services, you can give a tip to a taxi driver,hotel employees and even tour guides .

8. Haggling: In smaller shops or markets haggling is a normal thing over there. Feel free to bargain costs as it's normal as long as its done in a respectful and mutual way.

9. Language: Although English is widely spoken in Alanya, it is welcomed if you can pick up a few Turkish expressions. For easy navigation,favours,friendliness , it's important to learn few of the native language

10. Ramadan: Honor Muslims who are fasting if your visit falls during the month of Ramadan. Try not to drink,smoke or eat in the day time publicly. There are some restaurants that are closed In this period but there are the ones that serves visitors as well.

You may respect Alanya's culture and traditions and have a more enjoyable and culturally enriching vacation if you are aware of the local etiquette and customs.

CHAPTER 4

ALANYA TRAVEL TIPS

Certainly! Alanya is a beautiful coastal city in Turkey with a rich history and stunning landscapes. The following are few tips to help you enjoy your trip in alanya.

1. Best Time to Visit: The best time to visit Alanya is during the spring and autumn when the weather is pleasant. Summers can be scorching, and winters are mild.

2. Must-See Attractions:

   - Alanya Castle: Explore the historic castle with its breathtaking views.

   - Cleopatra Beach: Enjoy the famous sandy beach named after Cleopatra.

- Red Tower: Visit this iconic symbol of Alanya's maritime history.

- Damlatas Cave: Discover the impressive stalactites and stalagmites.

3. Local Cuisine: Don't miss out on trying traditional Turkish dishes like kebabs, baklava, and Turkish delight. Alanya also offers a variety of fresh seafood.

4. Shopping: Explore the local markets and bazaars for souvenirs, textiles, spices, and jewelry. The Alanya Bazaar is a popular spot.

5. Outdoor Activities: Alanya offers plenty of outdoor adventures, including water sports, boat trips, and hiking in the Taurus Mountains.

6. Currency: The currency used in Alanya is the Turkish Lira (TRY). Try to carry some cash with you incase you need to buy little items.

7. Language: Turkish is the primary language spoken in Alanya. While many people in the tourism industry speak English, it's helpful to know a few basic Turkish phrases.

8. Safety: Alanya is generally a safe destination for tourists, but it's wise to take standard precautions, like safeguarding your belongings.

9. Transportation: Getting around is easy with taxis, buses, and dolmuses (shared minibusses). Consider renting a car for more flexibility.

10. Respect Local Customs: While Alanya is a popular tourist destination, it's important to respect local customs and dress modestly when visiting mosques or more conservative areas.

Remember to check the latest travel advisories and entry requirements before your trip, as these can change. Enjoy your journey to Alanya!

WEATHER AND PACKING TIPS

When packing for a trip to Alanya, it's essential to consider the weather and your planned activities. Alanya has a Mediterranean climate with hot, dry summers and mild, wet winters. Here are some packing tips based on the season you plan to visit:

Spring (March to May):

- Weather: Spring in Alanya is pleasant, with temperatures ranging from 15°C to 25°C (59°F to 77°F).

- Packing List:

  - Clothings that are light and can let in air, like T-shirts, shorts, and sunwears.

  - Comfortable walking shoes for exploring.

  - Sunscreen and a wide-brimmed hat for sun protection.

  - Swimwear for the beach.

- A jacket that's light or a thicker sweater for evenings that are cold.

Summer (June to August):

- Weather: Summers in Alanya can be scorching, with temperatures often exceeding 30°C (86°F).

- Packing List:

  - Lightweight and loose-fitting clothing, such as tank tops and shorts.

  - Sunscreen, sunglasses, and a sunhat.

  - Swimwears, since you will likely be spending time at the beach.

  - Sandals or flip-flops for the hot weather.

  - Water bottle for when you are feeling testy.

  - Insect repellent.

Autumn (September to November):

- Weather: Autumn is still warm in Alanya, with temperatures between 20°C and 30°C (68°F to 86°F).

- Packing List:

  - Light clothing, including long sleeves for cooler evenings.

  - Comfortable walking shoes for outdoor activities.

  - Swimsuit if you plan to swim in the sea.

  - Light rain jacket or umbrella, as there may be occasional showers.

Winter (December to February):

- Weather: Winters in Alanya are mild, with temperatures around 10°C to 15°C (50°F to 59°F).

- Packing List:

  - Layered clothing, including sweaters, a light jacket, and long pants.

- Closed-toe shoes or boots for cooler weather.

- An umbrella and a compact travel umbrella.

- A few warm clothing items for cooler nights.

Make sure you check the weather forecast when it draws near to your travel dates for better packing guidance. Additionally, don't forget to pack any specific items you might need for activities like hiking, water sports, or cultural excursions. It's a good idea to pack travel sized toiletries and any necessary medications as well. Enjoy your trip to Alanya!

GETTING AROUND IN ALANYA

Getting around the city of Alanya is relatively easy, and there are several transportation options available to explore the area:

1. Walking: Alanya's city center is compact and pedestrian-friendly. You can easily explore the historic sites, markets, and beach areas on foot. A good way to savour the local atmosphere is by walking.

2. Public Buses: Alanya has a well-connected public bus system. You can use these buses to reach various parts of the city and nearby towns. Look for "dolmuş" (shared minibus) routes or municipal buses. The routes are usually marked clearly.

3. Taxi: Taxis are readily available in Alanya and are a convenient way to get around. Make sure the taxi driver uses the meter or agree on a fare before starting your journey. Taxis are especially useful for reaching destinations not covered by buses.

4. Car Rental: If you want more flexibility and plan to explore the surrounding areas, you can rent a car. Be sure to have the necessary documentation, and familiarize yourself with local traffic rules and parking regulations.

5. Bicycle Rental: Some areas in Alanya offer bicycle rental services. This can be a fun way to explore the city at your own pace, especially along the coastline.

6. Scooter Rental: Scooter or motorbike rental is another popular option for getting around Alanya. It's important to have a valid driver's license and follow local traffic regulations.

7. Boat and Water Taxis: Alanya's coastline is stunning, and you can use boat taxis or tours to explore nearby bays and beaches. This is a unique way to see the city from the sea.

8. Walking Tours: Consider joining guided walking tours to learn more about Alanya's history and culture. They are often led by guides with vast knowledge.

When using public transportation, it's a good idea to have local currency (Turkish Lira) for bus fares and small purchases. Also, remember to check the schedules and routes in advance, especially for buses and boats, as they may operate on specific timetables. Enjoy your travels around Alanya!

COMMUNICATION AND INTERNET IN ALANYA

Communicating and accessing the internet in Alanya, Turkey, is relatively straightforward. Here's what you need to know:

Mobile Phone Usage:

- You can use your mobile phone in Alanya if you have an international roaming plan, but be aware that roaming charges can be expensive.

- A more cost-effective option is to purchase a local Turkish SIM card. You can find them at airports, mobile shops, or kiosks. Some popular mobile operators in Turkey include Turkcell, Vodafone, and Türk Telekom.

Wi-Fi Availability:

- Many hotels, restaurants, cafes, and public spaces in Alanya offer free Wi-Fi. It's a good idea to ask for the Wi-Fi password or look for signs indicating its availability.

- Keep in mind that the quality of Wi-Fi can vary, and it may be slower in more remote areas.

Internet Cafes:

- While less common today, you can still find internet cafes in Alanya, which offer computer access and internet connectivity for a fee.

Communication Apps:

- If you have access to the internet, you can use popular communication apps like WhatsApp, Skype, and Viber to make voice and video calls. These apps are often used for international communication and are widely accessible in Alanya.

Emergency Services:

- The emergency number in Turkey is 112 for medical, police, or fire assistance. It's free to call.

Language:

- Turkish is the primary language spoken in Alanya, so having a translation app or a basic Turkish phrasebook can be helpful for communication.

Currency for SIM Cards:

- Make sure to have some Turkish Lira (TRY) on hand when purchasing a local SIM card or using pay-as-you-go services.

Internet Quality:

- In urban areas like Alanya's city center, you can generally expect decent internet speeds. However, in more remote or rural areas, the quality may be slower or less reliable.

Internet censorship:

- Turkey has implemented some internet restrictions, and certain websites and social media platforms may be temporarily blocked. Be aware of this and consider using a Virtual Private Network (VPN) if you need unrestricted access to the internet.

Overall, staying connected and accessing the internet in Alanya is quite convenient, whether you prefer to use your mobile phone, Wi-Fi, or internet cafes.

USEFUL PHRASES IN ALANYA

Learning a few basic Turkish phrases can enhance your travel experience in Alanya and help you communicate with locals. Below are few phrases that will be helpful over there:

1. **Merhaba** (Mehr-HAH-bah) - Hello

2. **Teşekkür ederim** (Teh-shehk-KOOR ed-EH-rim) - Thank you

3. **Lütfen** (Loot-fen) - Please

4. **Evet** (EH-vet) - Yes

5. **Hayır** (Ha-YUHR) - No

6. **Günaydın** (Goo-NAH-ydun) - Good morning

7. **İyi öğlenler** (EE-yee oh-LEHN-lair) - Good afternoon

8. **İyi akşamlar** (EE-yee ak-SHAHM-lar) - Good evening

9. **Hoş geldiniz** (Hosh gel-DUHN-iz) - Welcome

10. **Ne yapıyorsunuz?** (Neh yap-YUH-yor-sunuz) - What are you doing?

11. **Nerede?** (Nehr-ED-eh) - Where?

12. **Benim adım [Your Name].** (BEH-nim ah-DUHM [Your Name]) - My name is [Your Name].

13. **Bir bira, lütfen.** (Beer bee-RAH, loot-FEN) - One beer, please.

14. **Su** (Soo) - Water

15. **Nasıl gidiyor?** (Nah-SUHL gee-DEE-yor) - How are you?

16. **Ben turistim.** (BEHN too-REEST-im) - I am a tourist.

17. **Ben yardım istiyorum.** (BEHN yar-DUHM is-TEE-yor-um) - I need help.

18. **Kaç para?** (Kahch pah-RAH) - How much does it cost?

19. **Ben anlamıyorum.** (BEHN ahn-lah-MYOR-um) - I don't understand.

20. **Hesap lütfen.** (Heh-SAHHP loot-FEN) - Check, please.

Learning and using these basic phrases can go a long way in establishing rapport with locals and making your stay in Alanya more enjoyable. Turkish people often appreciate visitors who make an effort to communicate in their language.

Here are some more useful Turkish phrases to help you during your visit to Alanya:

21. **Beni anlayabiliyor musunuz?** (BEH-nee ahn-LAH-yah-bee-lee-yor moo-SOON-ooz) - Can you understand me?

22. **Bana yardım eder misiniz, lütfen?** (BAH-nah yar-DUHM ed-AIR mee-SEE-niz, loot-FEN) - Can you help me, please?

23. **Nerede tuvalet?** (Nehr-ED-eh too-VAH-let) - Where is the restroom?

24. **Hesap dahil mi?** (Heh-SAHHP dah-HEEL mee) - Is it included in the bill?

25. **Ben buraya nasıl giderim?** (BEHN boo-RAH-yah nah-SUHL gee-DAY-reem) - How do I get to this place?

26. **Bir şey önerir misiniz?** (Beer shay urn-AIR mee-SEE-niz) - Can you recommend something?

27. **Ne zaman açılıyor/kapanıyor?** (Neh zah-MAHN ah-chuh-LUH-yor/kah-pah-NUH-yor) - When does it open/close?

28. **Bir dakika, lütfen.** (Beer dah-KEE-kah, loot-FEN) - One moment, please.

29. **Sağlık olsun!** (SAH-uh-luhk ohl-SOON) - Bless you! (after someone sneezes)

30. **Nasıl giderseniz?** (Nah-SUHL gee-DEHR-sehn-iz) - However you like it. (polite response to "Teşekkür ederim")

31. **Beni Alanya Kalesi'ne götürün, lütfen.** (BEH-nee Ah-LAHN-yah Kah-LEH-see-neh goh-TOO-roon, loot-FEN) - Take me to Alanya Castle, please.

32. **Ani rica ederim.** (AH-nee ree-JAH ed-AIR-im) - You're welcome. (in response to "Teşekkür ederim")

Remember, making an effort to speak Turkish, even with basic phrases, can greatly enhance your travel experience and help you connect with the locals. Most Turks appreciate when visitors try to speak their language, even if it's just a few words.

Here are some additional useful Turkish phrases .

33. **Beni plaja götürün, lütfen.** (BEH-nee plah-jah goh-TOO-roon, loot-FEN) - Take me to the beach, please.

34. **Bir şişe su, lütfen.** (Beer SHEE-she soo, loot-FEN) - A bottle of water, please.

35. **İyi tatiller!** (EE-yee tah-TEE-ler) - Have a good holiday! (use this to wish others a good time)

36. **Güle güle kullanın.** (GOO-leh GOO-leh koo-LAHN-uhn) - Enjoy your meal. (say this when someone is eating)

37. **Benim için sürpriz yapabilir misiniz?** (BEH-neem eech-EEN soor-PREEZ yah-pah-BEER mee-SEE-neez) - Can you make a surprise for me?

38. **Ben burada tatil yapıyorum.** (BEHN boo-RAH-duh tah-TEEL yah-POO-yor-um) - I'm on vacation here.

39. **Nasıl gidebilirim?** (Nah-SUHL gee-deh-BEEL-ee-reem) - How can I get there?

40. **Turist bilgileri merkezi nerede?** (Too-REEST beel-GEE-leh-ree mehr-KEH-zee nehr-ED-eh) - Where is the tourist information center?

41. **Hava nasıl?** (HAH-vah nah-SUHL) - How's the weather?

42. **Kaç saat açık?** (Kahch sah-AHT ah-CHUHK) - What are the opening hours?

43. **Bana yardımcı olabilir misiniz?** (BAH-nah yahr-DUHM-juhl oh-lah-BEER mee-SEE-neez) - Can you help me?

44. **Teşekkür ederim, çok naziksiniz.** (Teh-shehk-KOOR ed-AIR-im, chook nah-ZEEK-see-neez) - Thank you, you're very kind.

45. **Bu ne kadar?** (Boo neh kah-DAR) - How much is this?

46. **Yardım çağırın!** (Yahr-DUHM chah-OHR-uhn) - Call for help!

47. **Tatilin tadını çıkarın!** (Tah-TEEL-een tah-DUH-nuh CHOO-kah-reen) - Enjoy your holiday!

48. **Bir fotoğraf çekebilir misiniz, lütfen?** (Beer fo-TOH-rahf cheh-KEH-beel-EER mee-SEE-neez, loot-FEN) - Can you take a photo, please?

Remember to speak these phrases with a friendly and respectful tone, and don't be discouraged if your pronunciation isn't perfect. Your effort to communicate in their local language will be appreciated.

Here are a few more useful Turkish phrases to help you during your visit to Alanya:

49. **Hangi otobüs Alanya Kalesi'ne gider?** (HAHN-gee oh-toe-BOOS Ah-LAHN-yah Kah-LEH-see-neh gee-DAYR) - Which bus goes to Alanya Castle?

50. **Ben burada ilk defa.** (BEHN boo-RAH-dah eelk DEH-fah) - I'm here for the first time.

51. **Ben Alanya'da tatil yapıyorum.** (BEHN Ah-LAHN-yah-dah tah-TEEL yah-POO-yor-um) - I'm on vacation in Alanya.

52. **Alışveriş merkezi nerede?** (Ah-LUHSH-vair-ISH mehr-KEH-zee nehr-ED-eh) - Where is the shopping center?

53. **Ne zaman açıyor/kapanıyor?** (Neh zah-MAHN ah-chuh-YOHR/kah-pah-NUH-yor) - When does it open/close?

54. **Bana yardımcı olur musunuz?** (BAH-nah yahr-DUHM-juh oh-LUHR moo-SOON-ooz) - Can you help me?

55. **Hesap, lütfen.** (Heh-SAHHP, loot-FEN) - The bill, please.

56. **Türk kahvesi istiyorum.** (Turk kah-VEH-si is-TEE-yor-um) - I want Turkish coffee.

57. **Saat kaç?** (Saht kahch) - What time is it?

58. **Yardım istemiyorum, teşekkür ederim.** (Yahr-DUHM is-TEH-mee-YOHR-um, teh-shehk-KOOR ed-AIR-im) - I don't need help, thank you.

59. **Ben Alanya'da eğleniyorum.** (BEHN Ah-LAHN-yah-dah eh-LEH-nee-yor-um) - I'm having fun in Alanya.

60. **İyi yolculuklar!** (EE-yee yol-JOO-look-lahr) - Have a good trip! (use this when someone is leaving)

These phrases should be helpful for basic communication and making your stay in Alanya more enjoyable. Turkish people are generally friendly and appreciative when visitors try to use their language, even if it's just a few words.

Below are a few more useful Turkish phrases to aid you during your time in Alanya:

61. **Benimle İngilizce konuşabilir misiniz?** (BEH-neem-leh een-gee-LEEZ-jeh koh-NOO-shah-BEER mee-SEE-neez) - Can you speak English with me?

62. **Biraz daha yavaş konuşabilir misiniz, lütfen?** (BEE-rahz dah-hah ya-VAHSH koh-NOO-shah-BEER mee-SEE-neez, loot-FEN) - Can you speak more slowly, please?

63. **Görüşmek üzere!** (Goo-ROOSH-mehk oo-ZEH-ray) - See you later!

64. **Ne kadar sürer?** (Neh kah-DAR soo-RAYR) - How long does it take?

65. **Alanya'da gezilecek yerler nelerdir?** (Ah-LAHN-yah-dah geh-ZEE-leh-jeck YEH-ler neh-LEHR-deer) - What are the places to visit in Alanya?

66. **Ne zaman açılıyor, biliyor musunuz?** (Neh zah-MAHN ah-chuh-LUH-yor, bee-lee-YOHR moo-SOO-nooz) - Do you know when it opens?

67. **Benim için bir harita var mı?** (BEH-neem ee-CHEEN beer hah-REE-tah vahr muh) - Is there a map for me?

68. **Kaç kişi?** (Kahch kee-SHEE) - How many people?

69. **Ben bu yeri seviyorum.** (BEHN boo yeh-REE seh-VEE-yoh-room) - I love this place.

70. **Hangi otelde kalıyorsunuz?** (HAHN-gee oh-TEHL-deh kah-LUH-yor-soon-ooz) - In which hotel are you staying?

71. **Bir sandalye, lütfen.** (Beer sahn-DAH-leh, loot-FEN) - A chair, please.

72. **Ben bu yemeği denemek istiyorum.** (BEHN boo yeh-MEHK den-eh-MEHK is-TEE-yoh-room) - I want to try this dish.

73. **Ben bir tur gezisine katılmak istiyorum.** (BEHN beer toor geh-ZEE-see-neh ka-TUHL-mahk is-TEE-yoh-room) - I want to join a guided tour.

74. **Size iyi günler!** (SEE-zeh EE-yee GOON-lair) - Have a good day!

75. **Alanya'da nerede güzel bir restoran var?** (Ah-LAHN-yah-dah NEHR-eh-deh goo-ZEHL beer rehs-TAH-rahn vahr) - Where is a nice restaurant in Alanya?

Using these phrases will help you interact with locals, make inquiries, and navigate the city more effectively during your visit to Alanya. Enjoy your time exploring the beautiful city!

MAPS AND ITINERARIES

charts and schedules

You can use these general procedures to acquire maps and plan your route in Alanya:

1. Alanya's Research: Look up the best things to do and places to visit in Alanya first. The Red Tower, Cleopatra Beach, Damlatas Cave, and Alanya Castle are a few of the well-liked tourist destinations.

2. Services Mapped: To explore Alanya, you can use a variety of map services such as Apple Maps, Google Maps, or a specialized travel app like TripAdvisor. These apps allow you to input your destinations and instantly receive maps and directions.

3. Build Your Itinerary: Make a daily schedule based on your interests and the length of your visit. List the locations you wish to see every day.

4. Transportation: Plan your route through Alanya. whether it's via taking public transportation, walking, renting a car, or a combination of these ways.

5. Accommodations: Be careful to keep your lodging information close to hand in case you need to consult it.

6. Related Advice: Look for any events or advice from the locals while you're there. For this, local travel websites, blogs, and forums can be useful.

3-day Itinary For Alanya

This is an example three-day schedule for Alanya:

Day 1: Discover the Old Town

Morning: - Arrive to Alanya Castle to begin your day. Savor the expansive views of the Mediterranean Sea and the city.

In the afternoon, visit the Red Tower and take a look around its museum to learn more about Alanya's past.

- The evening:- Take a relaxing walk through Alanya's Old Town's winding streets (Kaleici). There are quaint stores, eateries, and buildings from the past.

Day 2: Beach Day

- Morning: - Take a leisurely stroll over the beautiful sands of Cleopatra Beach in the morning.

- In the afternoon, have a meal at a restaurant by the beach, go water sledding, or just relax in the sun.

- In the evening, stroll idly down the promenade by the shore and check out the neighborhood market.

Day 3: Relaxing in Nature

-In the morning, go to the Damlatas Cave, also called Alanya Dim Cave, which is well-known for its breathtaking stalactites and stalagmites.

-In the afternoon, have a leisurely supper at a nearby restaurant or take a cool plunge in the Dim River.

-In the evening, take a stroll around Alanya Harbor and dine on seafood at one of the eateries on the waterfront.

Understand that this is merely an example of an itinerary. There are many different activities available at Alanya, and you can tailor your schedule to suit your interests. Don't forget to sample some authentic Turkish food while you're there as well. Have fun while you're in Alanya!

Alanya's 5-Day Itinerary:

History and Culture Day 4

-In the morning, go to the Alanya Shipyard to explore the historic shipyard and learn about Alanya's maritime past.

-In the afternoon, spend time exploring the Ethnographic Museum, which has artifacts showcasing the customs and culture of the area.

-Evening: - Enjoy the lively nightlife with bars and cafes by taking a leisurely stroll around the waterfront.

This expanded itinerary includes a day trip to Side, which is around an hour's drive from Alanya, and offers a combination of historical, cultural, and natural experiences. Make sure you modify the schedule to fit your needs and speed. There are plenty of things to do in Alanya that you may tailor to your interests. Have fun traveling!

Alanya's 7-Day Itinerary

For a more thorough and laid-back experience:

Day 6: Exploration and Environment

-In the morning, embark on an exciting journey to Sapadere Canyon, a stunning natural wonder featuring a cool river. You can swim, explore the canyon, and take in the tranquil surroundings.

-In the afternoon, go to the Alanya Archaeological Museum to see historical items from the area.

- Evening:- Make your way to Dinek Hill to observe the city's sunset. It provides beautiful vistas.

Day 7: Leisure Day

-Morning: - Take a leisurely stroll around your preferred beach, be it Cleopatra Beach or a more secluded one, to decompress and rejuvenate.

-In the afternoon, take advantage of some last-minute souvenir shopping or visit the neighborhood markets.

-Evening: Conclude your trip to Alanya with a farewell supper at a neighborhood eatery, maybe paired with a traditional Turkish performance.

You will get the chance to explore Alanya's natural features, historical sites, and adventurous offerings in greater detail with this 7-day schedule.

Adapt the days to your interests, and don't forget to sample the regional food and fully engage with the local way of life. Enjoy an amazing experience in Alanya!

For a more thorough 10-day exploration of Alanya, here's the extended schedule:

Day 8: Sun and Water Sports

-Morning: - Try out some water activities in Alanya's beaches in the morning, like windsurfing, jet skiing, and parasailing.

-In the afternoon :enjoy a leisurely beach picnic or lunch at a coastal café in the afternoon.

-In the evening, take advantage of Alanya's exciting nightlife by visiting pubs, clubs, or a bonfire by the beach.

Day 9: Day of Adventure

-In the morning, have an off-road adventure and breathtaking tour of the Taurus Mountains on an ATV or vehicle safari.

-In the afternoon, take a tour of the Alara Castle and the community that surrounds it to get a feel for country life.

-In the evening, head back to Alanya and have dinner at a quaint Turkish eatery in the Old Town.

Day 10: Spa and relaxation

Morning: - Visit one of Alanya's respectable hammams or wellness centers to begin your day with a spa and wellness experience.

In the afternoon, savor your final day of relaxation by swimming and tanning by the sea.

Evening: Take a sunset dinner cruise along the coast to round off your adventure.

With this 10-day schedule, you may fully experience everything Alanya and the neighboring areas have to offer—from adventure and the outdoors to leisure and culture. Make sure to sample the cuisine, mingle with the amiable inhabitants, and appreciate this seaside treasure for all its splendor. Have fun while you're here in Alanya!

RESOURCES AND CONTACT INFORMATION

I can give you some general information on Alanya, Turkey's resources and contact details. But bear in mind that the information I know is based on data that was accessible as of January 2022, and that specifics might have altered since then. The following are important contacts and resources in Alanya:

1. **Emergency Services:**

- Police: 155

- Ambulance: 112

- Fire Department: 110th

2. Medical Facilities and Hospitals: +90 242 512 7000 for Alanya State Hospital

There are also private clinics and hospitals accessible.

3. Municipality: www.alanya.bel.tr is the official website of the Alanya Municipality. On their website, you may find the contact details for different departments within the municipality.

4. Tourism Information: +90 242 513 1210, Alanya Tourism Office

5. Transportation: Alanya Harbor for maritime information; Alanya Bus Station: +90 242 513 0708.

6. Tourist Police (to help with matters pertaining to tourism):

- Tourist Police of Alanya: +90 242 513 1421

7. Embassy or Consulate (if you require consular assistance): Get in touch with your nation's closest embassy or consulate.

The following websites are helpful for learning more about Alanya, Turkey:

1. Visit the official Alanya Tourism website: Check out Alanya's official tourism website, usually run by the municipality. This website frequently offers comprehensive details on events, lodging, sights, and more.

2. TripAdvisor: TripAdvisor is a well-known travel website where you can read reviews left by other customers on hotels, restaurants, and attractions in Alanya.

3. Alanya - Lonely Planet: Lonely Planet provides travel guides to many places, Alanya included. You can discover helpful details regarding the city's attractions, food, and lodging.

4. Expedia and Booking.com: These websites are excellent for making reservations for lodging in Alanya. Online booking, pricing comparison, and review reading are all available.

5. The weather in Alanya: To find out the current weather and forecast in Alanya, visit a weather website or app, such as AccuWeather or the Weather Channel.

6. Google Maps: Use Google Maps to identify specific points of interest in Alanya, as well as to explore the city and get directions

7. Forums Alanya: You can ask questions, get advice, and share experiences with other travelers by participating in online travel forums and communities, such as TripAdvisor's Alanya forum.

8. Local Websites for News and Events: To learn about current events, festivals, and activities taking place in Alanya, look for local news websites or event listings tailored to the city.

When utilizing these websites to plan your journey to Alanya, please remember to double-check the information and look for the most recent facts.

CONCLUSION

As you prepare to conclude your incredible journey through Alanya, it's time to reflect on the tapestry of experiences that this captivating destination has to offer. Alanya, with its rich history, natural beauty, and vibrant culture, has proven itself to be a treasure trove of adventure and relaxation.

From the awe-inspiring Alanya Castle that whispers secrets of centuries past to the tranquil embrace of Cleopatra's Beach, where the turquoise waters invite you for a refreshing dip, this destination has something for every traveler. The mystical depths of Damlatas Cave and the iconic Red Tower stand as testaments to the city's historical significance, while the Alanya Archaeological Museum unveils the stories etched in its artifacts.

Alanya's charm extends beyond its landmarks. It's a place where you can revel in thrilling water sports, embark on boat tours under a setting sun, and explore lush nature trails offering breathtaking vistas. When the stars illuminate the night sky, the city awakens with a vibrant nightlife that will keep you dancing until dawn.

Don't forget to savor the flavors of Turkish cuisine, from delectable kebabs to delightful street food, and immerse yourself in the bustling markets to uncover treasures to take home as memories of your Alanya adventure.

As your journey unfolds, remember the warm smiles of the locals, their welcoming hospitality, and the beauty of a place where tradition meets modernity in perfect harmony.

Alanya has woven its magic into your heart, and as you depart, it's not a farewell but an "until we meet again." This remarkable city has left an indelible mark on your soul, and the memories you've collected here will continue to beckon you back. So, whether it's the call of the ancient Alanya Castle, the gentle lull of the waves at Cleopatra's Beach, or the echoes of laughter in the bustling streets, Alanya will forever hold a piece of your heart. Until next time, safe travels and may your next adventure be as enchanting as this one. Alanya awaits your return.

Printed in Great Britain
by Amazon

35786838R00075